Comprehension

Pupil Book **Year 2**

Shelley Welsh

Features of this book

- Extracts from a rich variety of fiction and non-fiction texts.

- Questions split into three sections that become progressively more challenging:

Warm up

Test yourself

Challenge yourself

- 'How did you do?' checks at the end of each topic for self-evaluation.

- Regular progress tests to assess pupils' understanding and recap on their learning.

- Answers to every question in a pull-out section at the centre of the book.

Contents

The Sound Collector by Roger McGough

A stranger called this morning
Dressed all in black and grey
Put every sound into a bag
And carried them away

The whistling of the kettle
The turning of the lock
The purring of the kitten
The ticking of the clock

The popping of the toaster
The crunching of the flakes
When you spread the marmalade
The scraping noise it makes

The hissing of the frying pan
The ticking of the grill
The bubbling of the bathtub
As it starts to fill

The drumming of the raindrops
On the windowpane
When you do the washing-up
The gurgle of the drain

The crying of the baby
The squeaking of the chair
The swishing of the curtain
The creaking of the stair

A stranger called this morning
He didn't leave his name
Left us only silence
Life will never be the same

1. Read the poem out loud. What is the poem about?

2. What sound does the clock make?

3. What sound do the flakes make?

4. In the poem, what noise is made when you do the washing up?

5. Read the first verse again. Which word rhymes with *grey*?

6. Read the fifth verse again. Which word rhymes with *windowpane*?

7. Where does the sound collector put the sounds?

8. Which **two adjectives** describe the stranger's clothes?

9. Why do you think the frying pan makes a hissing sound?

10. Read the last line of the poem. Why do you think *Life will never be the same*?

How did you do?

Bed in Summer by Robert Louis Stevenson

In winter I get up at night
And dress by yellow candle-light.
In summer quite the other way,
I have to go to bed by day.

I have to go to bed and see
The birds still hopping on the tree,
Or hear the grown-up people's feet
Still going past me in the street.

And does it not seem hard to you,
When all the sky is clear and blue,
And I should like so much to play,
To have to go to bed by day?

1 Find and write **two** different words that are a colour.

2 What sound can be heard outside in the summer?

3 What does the writer see when he goes to bed in summer?

4 Do you think the poem was written through the eyes of an adult or a child? Explain your answer.

5 When do you think this poem is set – recently or a long time ago? Explain why you think this.

6 The writer says that in summer:

   I have to go to bed by day.

   What does he mean?

7 Which **adjective** does the writer use to tell the reader it's not fair to be in bed while it is still light outside?

How did you do?

The Pied Piper of Hamelin

Once upon a time, there was a town called Hamelin where the people had lots of fine food. Then one day, the rats came. The rats stole the food, made nests in the homes and chewed up clothing. Nobody could sleep because of the loud squeaking noises the rats made! The people asked the Mayor to do something. They simply *had* to get rid of the troublesome rats.

The Mayor – a beady-eyed man with a HUGE tummy – put up a poster offering a reward to anyone who could get rid of the rats. Very soon, a tall thin man came to the Mayor's chambers. The man had twinkling eyes, wore strange, old-fashioned clothes and was playing a flute.

"Your Honour," he said. "I am the Pied Piper. I will rid your town of rats if you give me a thousand gold coins." The Mayor agreed and the Pied Piper strolled off, blowing his flute.

In no time at all, hundreds of rats were following the Pied Piper through the town. The squeaking rats ran faster and faster, until the Pied Piper reached the river. There, he stopped – but the rats carried on, until every single one of them was swept away by the rushing water. Everyone cheered with happiness.

The Pied Piper went for his reward. However, the Mayor refused to keep his promise to pay him. The Pied Piper was furious. He strode through the streets, playing his flute, until all the children in the town were enchanted by the music and started to follow him. Toddlers and babies, boys and girls – laughing and dancing, they all joined the procession.

The Pied Piper reached the mountain on the edge of the town. He led the children through a secret opening in the middle of the mountain. In they skipped quite happily. Then, rocks and boulders crashed down to hide the opening and they were gone. Neither the children nor the Pied Piper were ever seen again.

1. Who are the **two main characters** in the story?

2. Give one reason why the people of Hamelin wanted to get rid of the rats.

3. Which **adjective** is used to describe the rats?

Test yourself

4. *Very soon, a tall thin man came to the Mayor's chambers.*

   What does the word *chambers* mean in this sentence?

   baths   tables   rooms   fields

5. Which picture below looks most like the Pied Piper?

   A   **B**   **C**

6. Which word below best describes the Mayor of Hamelin? Select **one**.

   untrustworthy   shy   honest   kind

Challenge yourself

7. How do you think the people of Hamelin felt after the children disappeared?

8. Read the sentences below and work out the order they happen in the story. Write the letters a to d to show the order of events.

   a. The Pied Piper gets rid of the rats.
   b. The Mayor promises to pay the Pied Piper if he gets rid of the rats.
   c. The children disappear with the Pied Piper.
   d. The rats come to Hamelin.

The Three Little Pigs

A long, long time ago there was a mother pig who had three little pigs. She was very poor, so she sent them off to seek their fortune.

The first little pig met a man with a bundle of straw. "Please can I have that straw to build a house?" asked the little pig. The man said yes, and the first little pig built his house.

Then along came a big bad wolf who knocked at the door and said, "Little pig, little pig, let me come in!" The little pig replied, "No, no, no! Not by the hair on my chinny chin chin!"

The wolf said, "Then I'll huff and I'll puff and I'll blow your house in." And so the wolf huffed and she puffed and she blew the house in, and she gobbled up the first little pig!

The second little pig met a woman with a stack of sticks. "Please can I have those sticks to build a house?" asked the little pig. The woman said yes, and the second little pig built his house.

Then along came the wolf who knocked at the door and said, "Little pig, little pig, let me come in!" The little pig replied, "No, no, no! Not by the hair on my chinny chin chin!"

The wolf said, "Then I'll huff and I'll puff and I'll blow your house in." And so the wolf huffed and she puffed and she blew the house in, and she gobbled up the second little pig!

The third little pig met a man with a load of bricks. "Please can I have those bricks to build a house?" asked the little pig. The man said yes, and the third little pig, who was very clever, built *his* house.

Then along came the wolf who knocked at the door and said, "Little pig, little pig, let me come in!" The little pig replied, "No, no, no! Not by the hair on my chinny chin chin!" The wolf said, "Then I'll huff and I'll puff and I'll blow your house in." And so the wolf huffed and she puffed, and she puffed and she huffed, but she could not blow the house in.

The wolf was furious with the little pig and said she would come down the chimney to get him. So the little pig made a big fire and placed a huge pot of water on it. As the big bad wolf came down the chimney, he took the lid off and in fell the wolf! The little pig boiled her up until she was all gone. Then he sat by the fire and lived happily ever after.

1. How many pigs are there altogether in the story?

2. Why did mother pig send the three little pigs off to seek their fortune?

Test yourself

3. Explain why the wolf was able to blow down the house of straw and the house of sticks, but not the house of bricks.

4. Why do you think the third little pig is described as *clever*?

5. Which word below best describes the wolf?

dangerous   **shy**   **smart**   **trustworthy**

Challenge yourself

6. How do you think mother pig might have felt after she found out what happened to the three little pigs?

7. Do you think 'The Three Little Pigs' is a true story? Explain your answer.

8. Can you think of any other stories where 'good' wins over 'bad'?

The Tiger Who Came to Tea by Judith Kerr

Once there was a little girl called Sophie, and she was having tea with her mummy, in the kitchen.

Suddenly there was a ring at the door.

Sophie's mummy said, "I wonder who that can be. It can't be the milkman because he came this morning. And it can't be the boy from the grocer because this isn't the day he comes. And it can't be Daddy because he's got his key. We'd better open the door and see."

Sophie opened the door, and there was a big, furry, stripy tiger. The tiger said, "Excuse me, but I'm very hungry. Do you think I could have tea with you?"

Sophie's mummy said, "Of course, come in."

So the tiger came into the kitchen and sat down at the table.

Sophie's mummy said, "Would you like a sandwich?" But the tiger didn't just take one sandwich. He took all the sandwiches on the plate and swallowed them in one big mouthful.

Owp!

And he still looked hungry, so Sophie passed him the buns.

But again the tiger didn't eat just one bun. He ate all the buns on the dish. And then he ate all the biscuits and all the cake, until there was nothing left to eat on the table …

He ate all the supper that was cooking in the saucepans … and all the packets and tins in the cupboard … and he drank all the milk, and all the orange juice, and all Daddy's beer, and all the water in the tap …

Sophie's mummy said, "I don't know what to do. I've got nothing for Daddy's supper, the tiger has eaten it all."

… Just then Sophie's daddy came home.

So Sophie and her mummy told him what had happened, and how the tiger had eaten all the food and drunk all the drink.

And Sophie's daddy said, "I know what we'll do. I've got a very good idea. We'll put on our coats and go to a café."

1. Does Sophie's mummy know who is at the door?

2. Why can't it be Daddy at the door?

3. What was the next thing the tiger ate after the buns?

4. After he had drunk all Daddy's beer, what did the tiger drink next?

5. Write two headings in your book:

   Tiger ate   **Tiger drank**

   Under each heading, write everything the tiger ate and everything he drank.

Test yourself

6. Which **three adjectives** describe the tiger's appearance?

7. What did Sophie's daddy suggest they do when he came home?

Challenge yourself

8. What would you do if a tiger knocked at your door?

How did you do?

The Little Red Hen

One day, Little Red Hen found some grains of wheat. "I can plant these seeds and they will grow into lots more wheat." She asked her friends Cat, Dog and Goose to help her.

"Not I," said Cat. "I've got mice to catch."

"Not I," said Dog. "I've got a bone to bury."

"Not I," said Goose. "I've got eggs to lay."

"Then I'll plant them by myself," said Little Red Hen.

The wheat grew strong and golden in the sun and the rain. "This wheat is ready to cut." She asked her friends Cat, Dog and Goose to help her.

"Not I," said Cat. "I'm cleaning my paws."

"Not I," said Dog. "I'm chasing my tail."

"Not I," said Goose. "I'm late for a date."

"Then I'll cut it by myself," said Little Red Hen.

Little Red Hen gave the wheat to the miller who ground it into flour. "Now I can make a loaf of bread," said Little Red Hen. She asked her friends Cat, Dog and Goose to help her. Nobody answered. They were all asleep. "Then I'll make it by myself," sighed Little Red Hen.

When the loaf was ready, Little Red Hen asked, "Who will help me eat my bread?"

"I will!" shouted Cat.

"I will!" screamed Dog.

"I will!" shrieked Goose.

"Oh, I don't think so," said Little Red Hen. "None of you helped me when I needed you."

"But you can't eat all that bread by yourself," they exclaimed.

"Oh, I've got help to do that," said Little Red Hen. "Here come my little chicks. They will help me eat the bread."

And they did.

1. Who are the **four main characters** in the story?

2. Write each event from the story in the correct order.

   a. grind the wheat

   b. cut the wheat

   c. plant the seeds

   d. bake the bread

3. What reason did Goose give for not helping Little Red Hen plant the seeds?

4. What reason did Dog give for not helping Little Red Hen cut the wheat?

5. Who ground the wheat into flour?

6. Why did nobody answer when Little Red Hen asked for help to make the bread?

7. Why do you think Cat, Dog and Goose suddenly wanted to help Little Red Hen?

8. Write the adjective that best describes Cat, Dog and Goose.

   hard-working   **lazy**   **helpful**   **kind**

9. How did the chicks help Little Red Hen?

Farmer Duck by Martin Waddell

There once was a duck who had the bad luck to live with a lazy old farmer. The duck did the work. The farmer stayed all day in bed.

The duck fetched the cow from the field.
"How goes the work?" called the farmer.
The duck answered, **"Quack!"**

The duck brought the sheep from the hill.
"How goes the work?" called the farmer.
The duck answered, **"Quack!"**

The duck put the hens in their house.
"How goes the work?" called the farmer.
The duck answered, **"Quack!"**

The farmer got fat through staying in bed, and the poor duck got fed up with working all day …

The poor duck was sleepy and weepy and tired.
The hens and the cow and the sheep got very upset.
They loved the duck.

So they held a meeting under the moon and they made a plan for the morning.

"Moo!" said the cow.

"Baa!" said the sheep.

"Cluck!" said the hens.

And *that* was the plan!

It was just before dawn and the farmyard was still. Through the back door and into the house crept the cow and the sheep and the hens …

They squeezed under the bed of the farmer and wriggled about … they banged and they bounced the old farmer about and about and about, right out of the bed … and he fled with the cow and the sheep and the hens mooing and baaing and clucking around him.

Down the lane … **"Moo!"**

Through the fields … **"Baa!"**

Over the hill … **"Cluck!"**

… and he never came back …

1 Name **three** tasks that the duck had to do for the farmer.

2 Why did the farmer get fat?

3 Write **two rhyming adjectives** that describe how the duck felt.

4 Why were the hens, the cow and the sheep upset?

5 Which **two adjectives** are used to describe the farmer in the story opening?

6 What does the word *dawn* mean in this sentence?

It was just before dawn and the farmyard was still.

Select **one** answer.

evening   **morning**   **afternoon**   **night**

7 Which words below tell you what the plan was?

Moo! Baa! Cluck!	Oink! Miaow! Woof!	Quack! Hissss! Purrrr!
A	**B**	**C**

8 What do you think the animals did after the farmer had gone?

9 What do you think will happen to the farmer?

How did you do?

The Bog Baby by Jeanne Willis

Long ago, when we were little, me and Chrissy did something bad.
We said we were going to Annie's house to play, but we didn't.
We went fishing. All by ourselves.
Which wasn't allowed.

Chrissy said there was a **magic** pond in Bluebell Wood.
It was only ever there in spring.
When it rained, it made a huge puddle in the dell and pond creatures came.
We could fish for newts, she said.

I won't tell if you won't. So we went.
We found the pond.
It was squelchy round the edge. We fished and fished, but we didn't catch a newt.
We caught something much better.

We caught a **Bog Baby**.
He was the size of a frog, only round and blue.
He had boggly eyes and a spiky tail and I do remember he had ears like a mouse.
He came swinging through the flower stalks and jumped into the water.
He floated up and down on his back, and sucked his toes …

When we stroked him, he flapped his wings. They were no bigger than daisy petals …
We put him in a jam jar, took him home and hid him in the shed.

He was **our** Bog Baby.
He wasn't meant to be a secret. We wanted to show Mum, but we daren't.
If we did, she'd know we didn't go to Annie's.

We made our Bog Baby a beautiful home in a bucket …
We loved our Bog Baby. Our friends loved him too …
We took great care of our Bog Baby.
At least, we tried. But he got sick. He didn't jump up and down any more. He went pale and his wings drooped …
Mum found us in the shed … We'd promised not to tell, but I blabbed.
Mum wasn't angry, though.
When she saw who was in the bucket, she smiled and her eyes went misty.
She said she hadn't seen a Bog Baby since she was little.
Please make him better, we cried. We love him **so much**.
I know, she said. But the Bog Baby is a wild thing. He doesn't belong here … If we really loved the Bog Baby, we had to do what was best for him.
No matter how much it hurt us.
That was **real love**.
That's why we let him go.

1 Where did the writer and Chrissy go that they should not have?

    to Annie's house   **to the pond**   **to the shops**   **to school**

2 What were the girls trying to catch?

    a newt   **a Bog Baby**   **a mouse**   **a frog**

Test yourself

3 Which **adjective** does Chrissy use to describe the pond in Bluebell Wood?

4 Which **verb** tells you what the Bog Baby did with his wings?

5 Where did the girls hide the Bog Baby when they arrived home?

6 Why didn't the girls tell Mum about the Bog Baby to begin with?

Challenge yourself

7 *We'd promised not to tell, but I blabbed.*

What does the word *blabbed* mean in this sentence?

    started giggling   **told the secret**   **began to cry**

8 If the Bog Baby could speak, what do you think he would say?

How did you do?

The Big Fib by Ross Asquith

Just before Show and Tell, Robbie really did feel ill.

"Please, Mrs Pine," he said. "My tummy feels as if it's on a merry-go-round and my head feels as if it's on a big dipper." And then he gave the most enormous sneeze.

A-TISH-OOOOO.

"Atishoo, you need a tissue!" Robbie's friend Calum said.

"It sounds as if you're in a funfair, but without the fun," said Megan.

"More like a walrus playing the bagpipes," Archie joked.

Everybody laughed. To Robbie it seemed that the loudest laugh of all came from Anna Simpson.

But he couldn't stop. He sneezed again, even louder.

Megan pretended to put up an umbrella and the whole class roared.

"Now, that's enough." Mrs Pine shushed the class. "I think you'd better go home, Robbie. I'll call your mum."

By the time Robbie's mum arrived at school, Robbie was sneezing every two seconds. He sounded more like a volcano than a boy.

"I'm sorry I didn't believe you," Robbie's mum said, as she tucked him into bed.

Robbie wished he hadn't sniffed the pepper. His nose was running like a waterfall and his eyes itched and dripped, and it was a lovely sunny afternoon and he was stuck in bed.

1. When does Robbie start to feel ill?

2. Who is Mrs Pine?

3. Which noun phrase does Calum use that rhymes with 'atishoo'?

4. Which verb does the writer use to show that the class laughed very loudly?

Test yourself

4. Why does Megan pretend to put an umbrella up?

5. Why do you think Robbie sounds like a volcano?

Challenge yourself

6. Robbie's mum is sorry that she didn't believe him. What do you think Robbie had told her before he went to school?

7. Why do you think Robbie sniffed the pepper?

8. Do you think Robbie deserved to be laughed at? Why/why not?

How did you do?

Owl Babies by Martin Waddell

Once there were three baby owls: Sarah, Percy and Bill. They lived in a hole in the trunk of a tree with their Owl Mother ... One night they woke up and their Owl Mother was GONE.

"Where's Mummy?" asked Sarah.

"Oh my goodness!" said Percy.

"I want my mummy!" said Bill.

The baby owls *thought* (all owls think a lot) –

"I think she's gone hunting," said Sarah.

"To get us our food!" said Percy.

"I want my mummy!" said Bill.

But their Owl Mother didn't come.

The baby owls came out of their house and they sat on the tree and waited.

A big branch for Sarah, a small branch for Percy and an old bit of ivy for Bill.

"She'll be back," said Sarah.

"Back *soon*!" said Percy.

"I want my mummy!" said Bill.

It was dark in the wood and they had to be brave, for things *moved* all around them.

"She'll bring us mice and things that are nice," said Sarah.

"I suppose so!" said Percy.

"I want my mummy!" said Bill ...

And the baby owls closed their owl eyes and wished their Owl Mother would come. AND SHE CAME.

Soft and silent, she swooped through the trees to Sarah and Percy and Bill.

"Mummy!" they cried, and they flapped and they danced, and they bounced up and down on their branch.

"WHAT'S ALL THE FUSS?" their Owl Mother asked. "You knew I'd come back."

The baby owls thought (all owls think a lot) –

"I knew it," said Sarah.

"And I knew it!" said Percy.

"I love my mummy!" said Bill.

Answers

Pages 4–5 'The Sound Collector'
1. a sound collector / someone who collects sounds
2. ticking
3. crunching
4. gurgle / gurgle of the drain
5. away
6. drain
7. in a bag
8. black and grey
9. Answers may vary. For example: Because it is hot; because someone is cooking something in it.
10. Because all the sounds have gone.

Pages 6–7 'Bed in Summer'
1. yellow and blue
2. grown-up people's feet in the street / feet in the street
3. birds (still hopping on the tree)
4. a child; accept an explanation that refers to any of the following: the writer wanting to play; reference to hearing grown-ups which means he clearly can't be one; the fact that he *has* to go to bed
5. a long time ago; explanations should refer to the fact that candles are used instead of electric lights
6. It's still light when he goes to bed.
7. hard

Pages 8–9 'The Pied Piper of Hamelin'
1. the Pied Piper and the Mayor
2. Accept an answer that refers to any of the following: rats stole the food; they made nests in the homes; they chewed up clothing; nobody could sleep because of the loud squeaking.
3. troublesome
4. rooms
5. C
6. untrustworthy
7. Answers may vary. For example: sad, angry.
8. d, b, a, c

Pages 10–11 'The Three Little Pigs'
1. four
2. Because they were (very) poor.
3. Straw and sticks are not heavy/strong, but bricks are.
4. Because he built his house out of bricks, which are stronger than straw or sticks, and because he thought of putting hot water under his chimney to trap the wolf.
5. dangerous
6. Answers will vary. For example: She might be very sad that the wolf gobbled up the first two little pigs, but happy that the third little pig was alive.
7. Accept an answer that refers to one of the following: no, because pigs can't build real houses; no, because wolves don't blow houses down; no, because pigs/wolves can't speak; no, because wolves don't climb down chimneys.
8. Answers will vary. For example: 'Little Red Riding Hood', 'Sleeping Beauty'.

Pages 12–13 'The Tiger Who Came to Tea'
1. no
2. Because Daddy has a key.
3. the biscuits
4. all the water (in the tap)
5.

Tiger ate	Tiger drank
sandwiches	milk
buns	orange juice
biscuits	beer
cake	water in the tap
supper (in the saucepans)	
packets	
tins	

6. big, furry, stripy
7. (put on coats and) go to a café
8. Answers will vary. For example: I would say "Hello"; I would be scared; I would say "Go away".

Answers

Pages 14–15 'The Little Red Hen'
1. Little Red Hen, Cat, Dog and Goose
2. c) plant the seeds; b) cut the wheat; a) grind the wheat; d) bake the bread
3. "I've got eggs to lay."
4. "I'm chasing my tail."
5. the miller
6. They were all asleep.
7. Because they were hungry / So they could eat the bread.
8. lazy
9. They helped her eat the bread.

Pages 16–17 'Farmer Duck'
1. The duck had to: fetch the cow from the field and the sheep from the hill, and put the hens in their house.
2. Because he stayed in bed all day.
3. sleepy, weepy
4. Because they loved the duck and they saw her working too much.
5. lazy, old
6. morning
7. A Moo! Baa! Cluck!
8. Answers will vary. Accept answers that show a sense of relief or happiness. For example: They had a party.
9. Answers will vary. Accept any suitable answer. For example: He will go to another farm.

Pages 18–19 'The Bog Baby'
1. to the pond
2. a newt
3. magic
4. flapped
5. in the shed
6. Because Mum would know they hadn't gone to Annie's house.
7. told the secret
8. Answers will vary. Accept suitable answers. For example: I want to go back to the magic pond. / You are nice, but I don't like being in a bucket. / I want my mummy.

Pages 20–21 'The Big Fib'
1. Just before Show and Tell.
2. The teacher / Robbie's teacher
3. a tissue
4. roared
5. To make fun of Robbie's sneezes which are like rain.
6. Because his sneezes are loud and the noise is like a volcano erupting.
7. That he was ill.
8. To make himself seem ill.
9. Answers will vary.

Pages 22–23 'Owl Babies'
1. (three) baby owls
2. night
3. She thought she'd gone hunting.
4. Answers will vary. Accept anything that might be found in a wood. For example: Spiders/ants/creepy crawlies/badgers/foxes.
5. Bill because he kept saying "I want my mummy!"
6. Answers will vary. Accept any suitable answer. For example: She went hunting. / She went to visit someone.
7. swooped
8. Accept any of the following: they cried, "Mummy!"; they flapped; they danced; they bounced up and down on their branch.

Pages 24–25 'The Great Kapok Tree'
1. the larger man
2. Chop! and Whack!
3. flowers
4. the heat (and hum) of the forest
5. scampered
6. bright and small; also accept squeaky
7. silently
8. Answers will vary. For example: I think he went home. / He didn't chop the Kapok tree because he realised the animals and creatures were special. / I think he carried on chopping the tree because he didn't care.
9. Accept pictures that show each creature/animal that lives in the Kapok tree (jaguar, tree frog, monkey, bee).

Answers

Pages 26–27 'Where the Forest Meets the Sea'

1. A forest. Also accept: an island / a special bit of seashore.
2. crocodiles and kangaroos
3. A bird; Reasons will vary. For example: Because they rise which means they are in the sky like a bird. / Because they squawk which is a sound birds might make.
4. a stream of water
5. **a.** vines and creepers
   b. They push through them.
6. old
7. a. you can go inside it
8. The writer follows the sound of the sea to get back to their father.
9. on a fire
10. People might cut it down/destroy it.

Pages 28–29 'Dear Greenpeace'

1. b. to ask them for some information about whales
2. salt water
3. (crunched-up) cornflakes and breadcrumbs
4. Arthur
5. he smiled
6. Accept one of the following: whales live in salt water; whales travel great distances each day; whales are migratory; whales don't get lost.
7. travel great distances
8. Answers will vary. For example: They might think she is wasting the salt.
9. Because he had understood the letter from Greenpeace. OR: He had decided to be migratory again.

Pages 30–31 'Dinosaurs'

1. information
2. about 65 million years ago
3. meat
4. plants
5. Accept any two of the following: Long necks; long tails; walked on four feet.
6. giant dragons
7. an asteroid
   an ice age
   volcanoes erupting

Pages 32–33 'Poles Apart'

1. summer
2. the ice cap
3. Because it is too cold.
4. It keeps them warm / insulates them.
5. sleeping deeply through the winter
6. Because it is the driest, coldest and windiest place on Earth.
7. Because our planet is getting warmer. / Because the ice caps are melting.
8. Accept answers where labels for the North Pole and South Pole, Arctic and Antarctic have been drawn accurately. If any pupil switches the North and South, that's fine too, but it's worth explaining why we usually put north at the top.

Pages 34–35 'How to Make Your Teacher Happy'

1. home-made cake
   a cheery 'good morning'
   water
   a chocolate brownie
   a cushion
2. tidy the art area
   hand out books
   sharpen pencils
3. The teacher might have talked too much.
4. Answers will vary. For example: To make sure you will not be late. / Because being on time is a good way of showing you respect someone.
5. tired
6. make the cushion fatter

Pages 36–37 'Dougal's Deep-Sea Diary'

1. a city under the sea
2. mermaids / mermaids and stuff
3. **a.** = 12.30pm
   b. = Sunday
   c. = 9.30am
   d. = Thursday
4. an ancient treasure chest
5. Because he swam all day. / Because he was in the water all day. / Because that is what happens when you are in the water for a long time.
6. To give Dougal a reward (for finding the treasure).
7. **ATLANTIS**! Pupils' descriptive sentences will vary.

Answers

Pages 38–39 'Wonderful Weather'
1. a weather forecaster
2. trees, grass, flowers, plants, water to drink
3. When the sun shines and there are water drops in the air.
4. **a.** yellow
   b. indigo
5. Look like: small lumps of ice. Sound like: hammering.
6. Wednesday and Thursday
7. Accept a picture that reflects understanding of the description in the text.

Pages 40–41 'Rainforests'
1. c. There is lots of food up there.
2. There is not enough light.
3. Accept any three from: giant centipedes, ants, frogs, spiders, lizards, tigers, elephants, orangutans, mice, snakes.
4. They have long arms.
5. leafy umbrella
6. c. They don't need to, as they can make their homes, food and clothes from materials in the rainforest. And they have their friends and family around them.
7. Answers will vary. For example: I think the first fact is more interesting because that is a long time for a raindrop to fall. OR: I think the second fact is more interesting because it's a funny name for a tree.

1 Who were Sarah, Percy and Bill?

2 At what time of day did Sarah, Percy and Bill discover their mummy was gone?

Test yourself

3 When she discovered her Owl Mother wasn't there, where did Sarah think she had gone?

4 *… they had to be brave, for things moved all around them.*

What sorts of things do you think might have moved all around the baby owls in the wood?

5 Who was the youngest baby owl? Why do you think that?

6 Where do you think the Owl Mother went?

Challenge yourself

7 Which **verb** describes how the Owl Mother flew back to her babies?

8 How do you know the baby owls were excited to see their Owl Mother?

How did you do?

The Great Kapok Tree by Lynne Cherry

Two men walked into the rainforest. Moments before, the forest had been alive with the sounds of squawking birds and howling monkeys. Now all was quiet as the creatures watched the two men and wondered why they had come.

The larger man stopped and pointed to a great Kapok* tree. Then he left.

The smaller man took the ax he carried and struck the trunk of the tree. Whack! Whack! Whack! The sounds of the blows rang through the forest … Chop! Chop! Chop! The man wiped off the sweat that ran down his face and neck. Whack! Chop! Whack! Chop!

Soon the man grew tired. He sat down to rest at the foot of the great Kapok tree. Before he knew it, the heat and hum of the forest had lulled him to sleep …

A bee buzzed in the sleeping man's ear: "Senhor*, my hive is in this Kapok tree, and I fly from tree to tree and flower to flower collecting pollen. In this way I pollinate the trees and flowers throughout the rainforest. You see, all living things depend on one another."

A troupe of monkeys scampered down from the canopy* of the great Kapok tree. They chattered to the sleeping man: "Senhor, we have seen the ways of man. You chop down one tree, then come for another and another." …

A bright and small tree frog crawled along the edge of a leaf. In a squeaky voice he piped in the man's ear: "Senhor, a ruined rainforest means ruined lives … many ruined lives. You will leave many of us homeless if you chop down this great Kapok tree."

A jaguar had been sleeping along a branch in the middle of the tree … Now he leapt down and padded silently over to the sleeping man. He growled in his ear: "Senhor, the Kapok tree is home to many birds and animals. If you cut it down, where will I find my dinner?" …

A child from the Yanomamo tribe who lived in the rainforest knelt over the sleeping man. He murmured in his ear: "Senhor, when you awake, please look upon us all with new eyes."

The man awoke with a start. Before him stood the rainforest child, and all around him, staring, were the creatures who depended upon the great Kapok tree. What wondrous and rare animals they were! …

The man stood and picked up his ax.

Warm up

1 Which man left the rainforest – the larger man or the smaller man?

2 What **two** sounds did the ax make as the man chopped the tree?

3 Where do the bees collect pollen from?

4 What made the man fall asleep?

Test yourself

5 Which **verb** is used to tell you how the monkeys came down from the canopy?

6 Which **two adjectives** describe the tree frog?

7 Which **adverb** is used to show how the jaguar went over to the sleeping man?

Challenge yourself

8 What do you think the man did *after* he stood up and picked up his ax?

9 Draw a picture of the great Kapok tree with all the creatures that want to save it from being chopped down.

How did you do?

Where the Forest Meets the Sea by Jeannie Baker

My father knows a place we can only reach by boat.

Not many people go there, and you have to know the way through the reef.

When we arrive, cockatoos rise from the forest in a squawking cloud.

My father says there has been a forest here for over a hundred million years.

My father says there used to be crocodiles here, and kangaroos that lived in trees. Maybe there still are.

I follow a creek into the rainforest.

I pretend it is a hundred million years ago.

On the bank of the creek, the vines and creepers try to hold me back.

I push through. Now the forest is easy to walk in.

I sit very still.

… and watch.

… and listen.

I wonder how long it takes the trees to grow to the top of the forest!

I find an ancient tree. It is hollow. Perhaps aboriginal forest children played here, too.

I climb inside the tree. It's dark, but the twisted roots make windows. This is a good place to hide.

It is time to go and find my father. I think I hear the sea. I walk towards the sound.

My father has made a fire and is cooking the fish he caught.

I like fish cooked this way. But then I feel sad because the day has gone so quickly. My father says we'll come here again someday.

But will the forest still be here when we come back?

1. Where do the writer and their father go by boat?

2. The writer's father said **two** animals used to live there. Name them.

3. What sort of creature do you think a *cockatoo* is? Give a reason for your answer.

4. The writer follows a *creek* into the rainforest. What do you think a creek is?

   a large black bear   **a footpath**   **a stream of water**

5. **a.** Which **two** things make it difficult for the writer to walk in the forest?

   b. How do they solve the problem?

6. *I find an ancient tree.*

   Which word below means the same as *ancient*?

   leafy   **small**   **old**   **tall**

7. The tree is *hollow*, which means:

   a. you can go inside it   **b.** it has fallen over   **c.** it has no branches

8. What does the writer do to get back to their father?

9. How does the writer like their fish cooked?

10. Can you think of a reason why the forest might not still be there in the future?

Dear Greenpeace by Simon James

Dear Greenpeace,
I love whales very much and I think I saw one in my pond today. Please send me some information on whales, as I think he might be hurt. Love Emily.

Dear Emily,
Here are some details about whales. I don't think you'll find it was a whale you saw, because whales don't live in ponds, but in salt water. Yours sincerely, Greenpeace.

Dear Greenpeace,
I am now putting salt into the pond every day before school and last night I saw my whale smile. I think he is feeling better. Do you think he might be lost?
Love Emily.

Dear Emily,
Please don't put any more salt in the pond, I'm sure your parents won't be pleased. I'm afraid there can't be a whale in your pond, because whales don't get lost, they always know where they are in the oceans. Yours sincerely, Greenpeace.

Dear Greenpeace,
Last night I read your letter to my whale. Afterwards he let me stroke his head. It was very exciting. I secretly took him some crunched-up cornflakes and breadcrumbs. This morning I looked in the pond and they were all gone! I think I shall call him Arthur, what do you think? Love Emily.

Dear Emily,
I must point out to you quite forcefully now that in no way could a whale live in your pond. You may not know that whales are migratory, which means they travel great distances each day. I am sorry to disappoint you. Yours sincerely, Greenpeace.

Dear Greenpeace,
Tonight I'm a little sad. Arthur has gone. I think your letter made sense to him and he has decided to be migratory again. Love Emily.

Dear Emily,
Please don't be too sad, it really was impossible for a whale to live in your pond. Perhaps when you are older you would like to sail the oceans studying and protecting whales with us. Yours sincerely, Greenpeace.

Dear Greenpeace,
It's been the happiest day! I went to the seaside and you'll never guess …

1 Why did Emily write to Greenpeace?

   a. to ask them to visit her pond

   b. to ask them for some information about whales

   c. to tell them she had found a goldfish in her pond

   d. to ask them for some salt for her pond

2 According to Greenpeace, what sort of water do whales live in?

3 Name **two** different foods that Emily gave the whale to eat.

4 What name did Emily decide to give the whale?

Test yourself

5 What made Emily think the whale was starting to feel better?

6 Give **one** reason why Greenpeace said there couldn't be a whale in Emily's pond.

Challenge yourself

7 Choose **one** phrase from below to complete the sentence:

Animals who are *migratory* …

live in salt water   **travel great distances**   **live a long time**

8 Why might Greenpeace think that Emily's parents would not be pleased about her putting salt in the pond?

9 Why did Emily think Arthur had gone?

How did you do?

29

http:// www.whatisadinosaur.com

Dinosaurs

Dinosaurs roamed our planet until they became <u>extinct*</u> about 65 million years ago. Scientists use <u>fossils*</u> to find out information about them.

Different types of dinosaur

Theropods, sauropods and stegosaurs were just three different types of dinosaur. Theropods were meat-eaters, or **carnivores**; the other two were plant-eaters, or **herbivores**.

<u>Theropods:</u> Meat-eaters; powerful legs, short arms

<u>Sauropods:</u> Long necks and tails; walked on four feet

<u>Stegosaurs:</u> Slow; bony plates or spikes

How did dinosaurs became extinct?

1   Some scientists believe a massive <u>asteroid*</u> hit the Earth which caused the climate to change. This destroyed the plants that the herbivores ate so they died; then the meat-eating dinosaurs had nothing to eat so they died too.

2   Other scientists think there might have been an ice age which would mean the Earth would have been too cold for plants to survive, so the dinosaurs had nothing to eat and therefore died.

3   There might have been a lot of volcanic activity, which would have caused climate change. Again, the dinosaurs would not have been able to survive if plants were destroyed.

Did you know?

• The name dinosaur means 'terrible lizard' or 'frighteningly big lizard'.

• When dinosaur bones were first found hundreds of years ago, people thought they were the bones of giant dragons.

• An adult dinosaur weighed about 7 tonnes – that's the same as 250 seven-year-old children!

• Turtles, lizards, snakes, crocodiles and birds are all descended from dinosaurs.

Glossary

*   extinct: none of these life forms are alive any longer; they have all died out or been killed

*   fossil: the remains of a plant or animal that lived long ago, imprinted in rock

*   asteroid: a lump of rock moving around in space. Sometimes asteroids come down to earth with a bump. This can make a HUGE explosion.

1 What type of text is 'Dinosaurs'?

poem   information   instruction   story

2 When did dinosaurs become extinct?

about 6 million years ago   about 65 million years ago

about 6 thousand years ago

3 What did theropods eat?

4 What do herbivores eat?

Test yourself

5 Name **two** features of sauropod dinosaurs.

6 What did people think dinosaur bones belonged to when they first found them?

Challenge yourself

7 Write the bullet points that complete this sentence in your book.

Dinosaurs might have become extinct due to one or more of the following reasons:

- _____

- _____

- _____

How did you do?

Poles Apart

The Arctic and Antarctic

The Arctic and the Antarctic are located in the very north and

very south of the Earth. In the summer, it is light for 24 hours a day and in the winter it is dark for 24 hours a day. Both places have just two seasons – summer and winter (although summer is normally cold, compared to most places).

The North Pole is in the Arctic and the South Pole is in the Antarctic. There is a large area of ice around the Poles. Around the North Pole the ice floats on the Arctic Ocean, and at the South Pole a thick mass of ice known as an **ice cap*** covers the mountains of the land called Antarctica.

The land around the Arctic Ocean, called the **tundra***, is nearly always frozen. The top of it thaws in the summer months so grass can grow, but it is too cold for trees to grow.

Antarctica is the driest, coldest and windiest place on Earth. Not one person lives there, though researchers travel to the area and stay for months at a time, even through the 6-month darkness of winter!

Polar Animals

Most polar animals are **carnivores***. They hunt for fish and smaller animals. Animals in polar habitats have had to **adapt*** to survive the extreme cold. They keep warm by:

- having a thick layer of fat
- growing thick fur all over their body and feet
- having thick layers of feathers
- burrowing into the snow to make nests or caves
- **hibernating*** during the coldest months
- **migrating*** during the coldest months.

Thick fur

Our planet is gradually becoming warmer, which is causing the ice caps to melt. This means that some animals that live and hunt on the ice caps, like the polar bear in the Arctic, are becoming **endangered***.

Glossary

* ice cap: the ice that covers Antarctica and Greenland; it can be over a kilometre thick
* tundra: frozen, treeless ground in lands that are not quite as cold as Greenland
* carnivores: meat-eaters; many of them eat plants as well, for medicine
* adapt: adjust or change. If an animal adapts fast enough to change, it may survive.
* hibernating: sleeping deeply through the winter to cope with the hard conditions
* migrating: moving from one place to another to cope with winter
* endangered: at risk of dying out. The conservation organisation the WWF has a list of the animals that are endangered, vulnerable and threatened, and keeps it updated.

Warm up

1. In which season is it light for 24 hours in the polar regions?

   summer　　　　**autumn**　　　　**spring**　　　　**winter**

2. What is the name of the frozen mass covering the land in Antarctica?

3. Why don't trees grow in the tundra?

Test yourself

4. Why does growing a thick layer of feathers help birds to survive in the polar regions?

5. What does *hibernation* mean?

Challenge yourself

6. Why do no people live in the Antarctic all the time?

7. Why are some animals in the Arctic and Antarctic becoming endangered?

8. Draw a circle in your book. Draw an arrow to the top of your circle and another arrow to the bottom. Beside each arrow, write a label, one for the North Pole and the Arctic, and another for the South Pole and the Antarctic.

How did you do?

How to Make Your Teacher Happy

You will need:

- A teacher
- Some pupils
- Water
- Home-made cake
- A chocolate brownie

1   First, enter the classroom *on time* with a bright, sunny smile, and cheerfully wish your teacher good morning.

2   Then kindly offer to help your teacher prepare for the day ahead. Consider:

- tidying the art area
- handing out books
- sharpening pencils.

3   Next, carefully plump up the cushion on your teacher's chair. It is essential that your hard-working teacher is relaxed and comfortable at all times.

4   After that, politely ask your teacher if they would like a drink of water; your teacher is bound to be extremely thirsty from talking so much. (Try not to serve it in a dirty beaker from the art area.)

5   Then generously offer your teacher a piece of your mum's delicious home-made cake from your lunch box. It is a well-known fact that teachers are always hungry.

6   Finally, give your exhausted teacher a break from talking by calmly reading them a story at the end of the day. (You don't want your teacher to lose their voice.)

> **Top tips!**
> - Listen carefully in all lessons.
> - Line up sensibly when leaving the room.
> - Never forget to bring your PE kit.

> Warning: If your poor teacher falls asleep, wake them gently by placing a chocolate brownie on their knee. **NEVER USE A FAKE SPIDER!**

1 From the list below, select **five** items that are needed to keep your teacher happy, and write them in your book.

- some books
- home-made cake
- a cheery 'good morning'
- a fake spider
- a chocolate brownie
- a chair
- a head teacher
- pencils
- water
- a cushion

2 Which **three** things could you do to help your teacher prepare for the day ahead?

3 Why might your teacher be thirsty?

Test yourself

4 Look at Step 1:

*First, enter the classroom **on time** …*

Why do you think the writer has stressed the words *on time*?

5 In Step 6, the teacher is described as *exhausted*.

Can you think of another **adjective** that is similar in meaning to *exhausted*?

Challenge yourself

6 *… plump up the cushion on your teacher's chair.*

What do you think *plump up* means?

make the cushion fatter   **flatten down the cushion**

fold the cushion in two

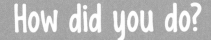

Diary writing

Dougal's Deep-Sea Diary by Simon Bartram

Friday

7.30am   I woke with excitement. I can't wait till tomorrow …

12.30pm   Lunch – too excited to eat (almost!) …

9.00   I packed my bags and went to bed early. Tomorrow I, little old Dougal, will become … **Dougal the deep-sea diver!**

Saturday

8.00am   I set off on the long coach trip to the harbour. On the way I read about a city under the sea called Atlantis – **WOW! Imagine that!** Full of mermaids and stuff. I wish I could go there …

Sunday

12.01pm   My first dive of the week. It was beautiful. So many fishy friends swam up to see me … I swam all day until my skin went wrinkly …

Wednesday

10.42am   **WOW!**
On my first dive today I found an ancient treasure chest hidden in an old shipwreck. Inside were mostly coins (too old to use) … and some hand-drawn maps of mysterious underwater worlds …
What a fantastic morning! …

Thursday

8.13am   I was woken by sounds of excitement in the harbour …
What a surprise!
The King and Queen were there and a beautiful new submarine glistened in the sea.
"In return," said the King, "for recovering the long-lost treasure of our land, I now present you with this beautiful reward." …

9.30am   The crowds cheered as I climbed into the sub and disappeared deeper into the sea than I'd ever been before.

11.02   I remembered the old maps and had a quick peek. I was sure no one would mind. I followed their directions all day and all night until …

Friday

8.29pm   **WOW!**
There it was. I couldn't believe my eyes!
It was real …

1. What is *Atlantis*?

2. Name something that Dougal says you might see in Atlantis.

Test yourself

3. Write the missing times and days for a, b, c and d in your book.

a.	Friday		Dougal has lunch
b.		12.01pm	Dougal's first dive
c.	Thursday		Dougal goes off in the sub
d.		11.02	Dougal remembers the maps

4. What did Dougal find on his first dive on Wednesday?

5. Why do you think Dougal's skin went wrinkly?

6. Why did the King and Queen visit Dougal on Thursday at 8.13am?

Challenge yourself

7. Read Dougal's last diary entry:

8.29pm **WOW!**

There it was. I couldn't believe my eyes!

It was real …

What do you think Dougal saw? Write the word in big, bold letters in your book, followed by an exclamation mark. Write a sentence to show what it might look like.

How did you do?

Wonderful Weather

There are lots of different types of weather. Weather can sometimes be unpredictable, but weather forecasters are usually able to tell us what the weather will be like over the next few days.

Lightning Facts
- Lightning can travel at a speed of up to 136,000 miles an hour.
- Lightning can reach a temperature of 30,000°C, which is hotter than the surface of the sun.

It's Raining, It's Pouring, The Old Man's Snoring
Rain falls as drops of water from the clouds in our sky. Don't grumble about rain – without it, we wouldn't have trees, grass, flowers, plants or drinking water!

Rainy Rainbows
When the sun shines and there are water drops in the air, we often see a rainbow. The colours always appear in the same order: red, orange, yellow, green, blue, indigo and violet.

Lively Lightning
Lightning is a very bright flash of electricity that happens in a thunderstorm.

Twisted Tornadoes
A tornado is a very violent windstorm. It looks like an elephant's grey trunk, swaying from the sky towards the ground. It can travel as fast as 500km per hour, destroying everything in its path, and sometimes lifting things up so that they drop to the ground elsewhere – frogs, fish, Dorothy's house …

Hammering Hailstones
Hailstones are small lumps of ice that fall from the clouds. They can make a very loud noise as they hammer on a roof.

Weekly Weather Chart
A good way of recording weather over time is in a chart.

Month: May Week: 1	Monday	Tuesday	Wednesday	Thursday	Friday	Saturday	Sunday
Weather observations	Sun and clouds; light wind	Morning: light showers; Evening: some sun, no wind	Heavy rain, strong winds; stormy overnight	Rain showers all day; evening sunshine	Cool morning; grey skies and light wind	Fresh start, then warmer	Much warmer; no wind.
Temperature	9°C	10°C	8°C	9°C	7°C	9°C	12°C
Rainfall	0cm	0.5cm	2cm	1cm	0cm	0cm	0cm

1. Who is usually able to predict what the weather will be like?

2. Name **five** things we would not have without rain.

3. When might we see a rainbow?

Test yourself

4. In a rainbow:
   a. Which colour comes after orange?
   b. Which colour comes before violet?

Challenge yourself

5. Describe what hailstones look like and what they sound like.

6. Look at the weather chart. Which **two** days would not be good for a picnic?

7. Read the paragraph about *Twisted Tornadoes*. Using the description to help you, draw a picture of a tornado as it destroys (or lifts!) houses and trees in its path.

How did you do?

Rainforests

What are rainforests?

Rainforests are found in places where there is a lot of rain. They are thick forests where very tall trees grow. The trees form a leafy umbrella which is called a canopy. A lot of animals live high up in this canopy because there is plenty of food there. The floor of the rainforest is dark and damp. There aren't many plants here because there isn't enough light. The largest rainforest is in the Amazon basin in South America.

People

The people who live in rainforests often make their homes, food and clothing from materials that can be found in the forest. Some of these people have no contact with the outside world – that's *us*!

Beasties

There are millions of different kinds of creatures in the rainforest: giant centipedes, ants, frogs, spiders and lizards are just some of them.

Animals

Tigers, elephants, orangutans, mice and snakes can all be found in rainforests. Orangutans have adapted to living there by having long arms so they can swing from tree to tree.

Food

A lot of the foods we eat, such as bananas and mangoes, come from rainforests. Some medicines that we need come from the plants found in rainforests.

Fun facts

* It can take 10 minutes for a falling raindrop to travel from the canopy to the rainforest floor!
* In Australia's Daintree rainforest, there is a tree called the **idiot fruit tree**!

1 Why do lots of animals live in the rainforest canopy? Choose a, b, c or d.

    a. There is no room on the floor.

    b. They like to lie in the sun.

    c. There is lots of food up there.

    d. They have good views.

2 Why don't many plants grow on the rainforest floor?

3 Name **three** creatures that you might find in a rainforest.

4 How have orangutans adapted to living in rainforests?

5 What **noun phrase** is used to describe what the rainforest canopy looks like?

6 Why don't some people in the rainforest have any contact with the outside world? Choose a, b or c.

    a. They don't know how to get out of the rainforest to the outside world.

    b. They don't speak the same language as people in the outside world.

    c. They don't need to as they can make their homes, food and clothes from materials in the rainforest. And they have their friends and family around them.

7 Re-read the two Fun facts. Which do you find more interesting, and why?

Notes page

Published by Keen Kite Books
An imprint of HarperCollins*Publishers* Ltd
The News Building
1 London Bridge Street
London SE1 9GF

ISBN 9780008244613

First published in 2017

10 9 8 7 6 5 4 3 2 1

Text and design © 2017 Keen Kite Books, an imprint of HarperCollins*Publishers* Ltd

Author: Shelley Welsh

The author asserts her moral right to be identified as the author of this work.

Series Concept and Commissioning: Michelle I'Anson and Shelley Teasdale
Contributor: Rachel Clarke
Project Manager: Fiona Watson
Editor: Caroline Petherick
Inside Concept Design: Paul Oates
Cover Design: Anthony Godber
Text Design and Layout: QBS Learning
Production: Natalia Rebow
A CIP record of this book is available from the British Library.

Acknowledgements
The author and publisher are grateful to the copyright holders for permission to use quoted material. Every effort has been made to trace copyright holders and obtain their permission for the use of copyright material. The author and publisher will gladly receive information enabling them to rectify any error or omission in subsequent editions.

Text © 1992 Martin Waddell.
From OWL BABIES by Martin Waddell & Illustrated by Patrick Benson
Reproduced by permission of Walker Books Ltd, London, www.walker.co.uk

Copyright © 1988 Jeannie Baker.
WHERE THE FOREST MEETS THE SEA by Jeannie Baker
Reproduced by permission of Walker Books Ltd, London, www.walker.co.uk

Copyright © 1991 Simon James
From DEAR GREENPEACE by Simon James
Reproduced by permission of Walker Books Ltd, London, www.walker.co.uk

Text © 1991 Martin Waddell
From FARMER DUCK by Martin Waddell & Illustrated by Helen Oxenbury
Reproduced by permission of Walker Books Ltd, London, www.walker.co.uk

Excerpt from THE GREAT KAPOK TREE: A Tree of the Amazon Rain Forest by Lynne Cherry. Copyright © 1990 By Lynne Cherry. Reprinted by permission of Houghton Mifflin Harcourt Publishing Company. All rights reserved.

Extract from *The Big Fib* Copyright © 2014 Ros Asquith
Published by permission of Barrington Stoke Ltd

The Tiger Who Came to Tea. Reprinted by permission
of HarperCollins*Publishers* Ltd © 1968 Judith Kerr

The Sound Collector by Roger McGough; taken from *All the Best – The Selected Poems of Roger McGough*.
©2004 Roger McGough. Published by Puffin and used by permission of Penguin Random House.

The Bog Baby by Jean Willis, published by Puffin. © 2008 Jean Willis.
Used by permission of Penguin Random House.

Text taken from *Dougal's Deep Sea Diary* by Simon Bartram Published by Templar Publishing. Text copyright ©2005 by Simon Bartram. Used by permission.

Images are ©Shutterstock.com and HarperCollins*Publishers* Ltd

HarperCollins
PUBLISHERS
— Since 1817 —
200